MY FRIEND IS
SUICIDAL

Bruce Ray

Consulting Editor: Dr. Paul Tautges

My Friend is Suicidal

© Bruce Ray 2014

Paper ISBN 978-1-63342-075-5
ePub ISBN: 978-1-63342-076-2
Kindle ISBN: 978-1-63342-077-9

Published by **Shepherd Press**
P.O. Box 24
Wapwallopen, PA 18660

www.shepherdpress.com

All Scripture quotations are from the New American Standard Bible (NASB). Copyright © 1995 by The Lockman Foundation.

Designed by **documen**

CONTENTS

INTRODUCTION
"TOO MUCH DEATH!"

We had responded to our third suicide call in less than a week when one of the detectives working the case, a veteran investigator, looked at me and muttered through clenched teeth, "Too much death!" Then, without another word, he turned and walked off the scene. I should have gone after him, but I didn't.

The questions that drove my detective friend away that day were also swirling around my own weary mind. What's going on? Why would Kathy, a friendly and popular employee of a local business, take her life on her lunch hour? Why did Jimmy, barely in his teens, end his life before it had really begun? And how could Matt, a loving husband and father, abandon his young wife and children when they needed him so much?[1]

We understand that people die. They die of old age and cancer. They die in traffic accidents and disasters and wars. We even understand that some people are victims of homicide. But suicide is different. Suicide is self-inflicted. Suicide is a choice. Why? Why do so many people today think suicide is the solution to their difficulties? I've had to think a great deal about suicide in the past twenty-plus years, and I've learned a great deal about suicidal subjects, too.

Suicide is not new. But its acceptability and even popularity are quite new. Early in the 20th century, Masaryk called suicide "a social ailment peculiar to modern society."[2] Only fifty years later, Myers labeled depression "the common cold of psychological disorders."[3] Today there are more than 36,000 confirmed suicides in the US every year (2009=36,909).[4] More than 101 people take their own lives every day; four every hour; one every fifteen minutes. That's "too much death!":

The actual numbers are underreported. For every completed suicide there are an estimated 25 attempts.[5] In 2006, there were almost 600,000 hospital Emergency Room visits attributed to suicide attempts.

That means there are a lot of friends who are suicidal!

Statistics like these provide useful information, but we must never forget that these numbers represent husbands and wives, mothers and fathers, sons and daughters, friends, neighbors, coworkers and classmates.

You picked up this book on purpose. You picked it up because you have been affected by the "ripples of suicide"[6] and you know that you will be affected again when another friend or loved one ends his or her life. You picked up this mini-book because you want to be able to help.

Suicide literature often distinguishes between suicide prevention, intervention and *post*vention. "Vention" comes from the Latin venire (to come) plus pre (to come before), *inter* (to come between) and *post* (to come after).

This booklet will address suicide prevention and intervention. It will help you to recognize the warning signs of suicidal thinking and to be able to defuse a suicidal subject before a suicide takes place. You have a good possibility of being successful. Those who work in the field tell us, "A significant number of suicides are preventable, provided help is available."[7]

Another book in this series, *Help! Someone I Love Has Committed Suicide*, will address suicide *post*vention: how to help family and friends ("suicide survivors") after a suicide has occurred.

1
What is Suicide?

Art Linkletter was a beloved radio and television pioneer in the '50s and '60s. Many of us will never forget his interviews of school children, "Kids Say the Darndest Things." Art Linkletter was also a suicide survivor. His daughter, a UCLA student, committed suicide by jumping out her sixth-floor kitchen window in 1969. In the foreword to *Ripples of Suicide* by police chaplain Harold Elliott, Linkletter wrote:

> The word "suicide" is without doubt one of the most dreadful expressions in the English language.
>
> People wince at the sound of it, and avoid using it to describe the tragic death it implies. Leprosy and Cancer are spoken of in the same hushed tones.
>
> And yet it must be faced squarely and discussed openly because it has become one of the leading causes of death among both the young and the very old in this country.

*No one can be sure of the exact figures
because suicides are deliberately
misreported and misdiagnosed as
an accident.*

*My own personal experience with it
is still a nightmare. The death of my
nineteen-year-old daughter, Diane, after
experimenting with LSD, changed my life
and the lives of everyone in my family.
We still find it difficult to understand
or discuss.*[8]

You never "get over" a suicide. Art Linkletter
wrote these words in 1993, 24 years after Diane's
death. He died in 2010, still grieving the loss of
his daughter.

Suicide is the *intentional* killing of oneself.
Accidental drug overdoses and other self-injurious
acts resulting in death that are determined to be
unintentional are not included in suicide statistics.
Suicide is often described as a permanent solution
to a *temporary* problem.

Navy Chaplain Gary Stewart reminds us that
suicide is the culmination of a process; it is seldom
provoked by just one unresolved problem. He
states, "Suicide is a permanent, intentional and
selfish action taken against one's self in order to

eliminate what for the moment appears to be unrelenting and unfaltering pain. It is a tragic culmination of a process in which unresolved events converge, leaving a person lonely, depressed, and thoroughly hopeless."[9] Security consultant Gavin de Becker agrees, "The process of suicide starts way before the act of suicide."[10]

Myths and Misperceptions

There are many myths and misperceptions about suicide that hinder us from dealing effectively with suicidal persons. Here are some of them, with brief comments:

> *Suicide is always caused by depression.*
> Actually, other factors such as anger,
> revenge, remorse and drug and alcohol
> abuse may be more dominant influences.
> Bill and Mary were a young couple who
> were living together. They went to a bar
> to celebrate a special occasion. Both had
> been drinking and Bill accused Mary of
> flirting with another bar patron. They
> argued all the way home, where Bill
> decided to show Mary how upset he
> was by forcing her to watch him commit

suicide in front of her.

People who talk about suicide won't really do it – they just want attention. It is true that sometimes suicide "attempts" are cries for help, but remember the boy who cried "Wolf!" One day the wolf actually came, and no one believed him. It is dangerous to assume that a suicide threat is "only" to get attention.

Thinking about suicide means you will commit suicide. Many people have fleeting occasional suicidal thoughts, but do not act on them. A key concern is when thinking about suicide extends to the point of actually making a plan.

If you talk about suicide to a suicidal subject, you may encourage her to do it. The fear of pushing someone over the edge leads us to avoid the subject. Actually, talking about her thoughts and feelings to someone who is really listening and interacting may be a release for the suicidal subject that makes it unnecessary for her to act.

A true believer cannot commit suicide. Samson was chosen by God to be one of the judges who would deliver and protect his people from the Philistines (Judges 13-16). Despite his many faults, Samson seems to have been a true believer who prayed for God to give him the strength to collapse the Philistine temple on his captors even though it meant his own death as well. Samson is named in "the great faith chapter" of the Bible (Hebrews 11) as one of many "who through faith conquered kingdoms, administered justice, and gained what was promised" (Hebrews 11:32-33)[11]. Other factors may affect the decisions believers make. Pastor Bob stunned everyone when he put a handgun to his head and pulled the trigger one night. Weeks later, his wife discovered that a new heart medication he was taking listed depression and suicidal ideation as possible side effects. If they had known, they could have removed all guns from the house as a precaution and discussed changing the medication with his cardiologist.

Suicide happens without warning.
Actually, most people give warning signs
that they are considering suicide. The
problem is that often we don't recognize
they were warning signs until after
the fact.

*Once suicidal, always suicidal. Not
true.* The primary value of a 72-hour
involuntary commitment by a mental
health professional is that it puts a
suicidal subject in a safe place and
enables him or her to get past a critical
period and reconsider other options.

*The risk goes down when the mood goes
up.* Not necessarily true. Actually, the
mood may seem to improve because a
decision has been made.

Suicidal people are intent on dying. More
often, suicidal persons want to end the
pain and think they are out of options
and out of hope. Not wanting to go
on living as you are is not the same as
wanting to die.

Suicide runs in families. That's often true, but that doesn't mean suicide is hereditary. It is more likely that family history provides unhealthy patterns of dealing with issues and "permission" to end life when solutions can't be easily found.

Someone who commits suicide must be mentally ill. Nevada's suicide prevention plan authoritatively declares, "90% of people who die by suicide have a diagnosable mental health and/or substance use disorder at the time of death." Only four sentences later, however, it acknowledges that "over 90% of the people that died by suicide in Nevada had not been seen by a mental health professional."[12] Then how were they diagnosed? This sounds like circular reasoning to me: "People who commit suicide must be mentally ill. Jenny committed suicide; Jenny must have been mentally ill." As we'll see later, that argument will quickly discredit you when talking with a suicidal subject.

Who Is at Risk and Why?

Who is at risk of committing suicide? Everyone. No one is immune. The group at highest risk of *attempting* suicide is white females. Women are ten times more likely to attempt suicide than men. However, the group at highest risk of *succeeding* is white males, ages 15-25 and 55-65. Why? Men generally use more lethal means of committing suicide, such as firearms. Why those ages? Both of those age groups represent periods of great change and transition. In the late teens/early twenties young people are trying to "find themselves" and figure out how they want to spend their lives and with whom. In the late fifties/sixties they are facing the end of careers, retirement, perhaps a failure to achieve certain life goals, and the prospect of declining health and finances. These can be dangerous times.

Why do people take their own lives? I've heard people give many explanations for contemplating suicide, and I've also read suicide notes in which people made their case for self-destruction, sometimes in great detail and other times in broad, rambling sentences. Here are some of the reasons people have given:

Anger

Jealousy

Depression – but consider this: "Not everyone who is depressed is suicidal, and not everyone who is suicidal is depressed. Bitterness, anger, and an unwillingness to forgive are common features of suicidal thinking."[13]

Self-pity

Pride

Shame

Guilt

Revenge

To avoid greater pain

Loneliness and isolation

Rejection

Loss of status, income, or power

Bored – "life has lost its meaning"

Autonomy – "I'll be the captain of my fate"

Divorce or the death of a spouse – "I can't live without him/her"

Bad relationships

Accidental – trying to achieve a different outcome, as in a drug overdose or sexual asphyxia

Stress

Bad theology – A teenage couple near Seattle were convinced that physical limitations and mortality are merely illusions that we ourselves create, an idea popularized by novelist Richard Bach.[14] When life proved disappointing, they thought they could just drop out of this illusory world and start over again by driving their Camaro through a brick wall at 110 mph. The wall was very real. One teen died on impact; the other survived but with critical injuries.

A chronic or terminal disease diagnosis. "The risk of suicide spikes in the weeks immediately following a cancer diagnosis, a new study shows. Patients were almost 13 times more likely to commit suicide in the first week after learning they had cancer than they were prior to the diagnosis. Twelve weeks after the diagnosis they were still nearly 5 times as likely to commit suicide as they had been before, according to the study published today in the New England Journal of Medicine."[15] Oregon and Washington both have physician-assisted suicide laws (PAS). Washington's Death with Dignity Act (2008) states, "The attending physician may sign the patient's death certificate which shall list the underlying terminal disease as the cause of death."[16] These suicides are not even counted as suicides!

One of the things to take away from a list like this is that all of these are reasons why people think about committing suicide. They may not be good reasons, or compelling reasons, but they are still reasons – and that means that suicide is not an unreasonable or irrational act. Remember this when you talk to your suicidal friend. Always show respect. Some suicidal persons have obvious mental distress, but the fastest way to lose your friend is to treat him like he's out of his mind and devalue his thoughts and emotions.

Another thing to recognize from a list like this is that none of these reasons is sufficient to explain suicide. These are the issues that people present, but they are not the reasons why they end their own lives. There is ultimately only one reason why people commit suicide. Most of them have not lost their minds, but all of them have lost hope. They have developed tunnel vision and cannot see any other workable options. Suicide is the only choice left that makes sense – i.e., the only option that to them seems *reasonable*.

2
Suicide and Scripture

On the surface, suicide is about death. If a suicidal subject succeeds in carrying out his or her plan, they will die. Family, friends and acquaintances will all mourn.

But that's on the surface. When we plunge deeper into the subject we may be surprised to discover that suicide is really about life and dissatisfaction with living.

Some people argue that the Bible doesn't speak to the issue of suicide, and that its silence implies approval. Medical ethics professor Dónal O'Mathúna acknowledges, "Nowhere does the Bible use the word 'suicide,' nor give a command against taking one's own life."[17] However, although the word is not used, that does not mean that the subject is not addressed. O'Mathúna notes that every major branch of Judaism and Christianity has historically viewed suicide as wrong. Suicide is generally treated as a violation of the sixth commandment, "You shall not murder" (Exodus 20:13).

The Origins of Suicide

To understand suicide, we need to go back to Genesis: "In the beginning God created..." (Genesis 1:1). From the beginning, the Creator distinguished himself from all the things that he made. Genesis 1-3 describe the origins of the first man, the first woman, the first marriage, the first family, the first work, the first sin, and the origin of spiritual and physical death.

Our first parents were tempted, not by a tasty fruit in the Garden, but by the prospect of being as gods themselves, of determining for themselves what is true and false, and right and wrong (Genesis 3:4-6). The issue for Adam and Eve was one of control and relationships: would they be content to trust their Creator and submit to his word, or would they attempt to usurp his authority and assert their own autonomy? Adam acted as the representative head of all mankind, and "in Adam's fall, we sinned all."

The apostle Paul explains, "... sin entered the world through one man, and death through sin, and in this way death came to all men, because all sinned..." (Romans 5:12). Death therefore is not "natural" as many portray it. Death is a consequence of sin and an enemy we face throughout life.

Suicide Denies God's Sovereignty

It is important to recognize that the time of our death has been appointed by God: "All the days ordained for me were written in your book before one of them came to be" (Psalm 139:16). The manner of our death has also been appointed by God. Jesus told Peter, "I tell you the truth, when you were younger you dressed yourself and went where you wanted; but when you are old you will stretch out your hands, and someone else will dress you and lead you where you do not want to go" (John 21:18). John explains, "Jesus said this to indicate the kind of death by which Peter would glorify God" (John 21:19).

What happens at death? The short answer is "the dust returns to the ground it came from, and the spirit returns to God who gave it" (Ecclesiastes 12:7). Solomon warns that we do not want to face death without first returning to a right relationship with our Creator (Ecclesiastes 12:1; 13-14).

When life is not what we want it to be, or think it should be, some consider ending it themselves. Suicides don't generally occur when life is going well, but when someone is depressed, disappointed, angry, or weary of struggling with difficult issues or relationships. Most suicidal people do not want to die. They want something in their life to change, but they don't know how to make that happen. Suicide then represents the ultimate act of self-determination and the rejection of God's sovereignty over all the circumstances of life.

Psychiatrist Thomas Szasz brazenly dismisses the rights of the Creator when he proclaims, "A man's life belongs to himself. Hence, he has a right to take his own life, that is, to commit suicide."[18] As John Ling argues, "Suicide is a personal assault against the sovereignty of God in all the affairs of human life. The suicide declares that she has a sovereign rule over her life and a sovereign reign over her death – neither of which is true. Our lives belong to God. He oversaw our conception, he gave us our first breath, he has sustained us, and he alone has the entitlement to take it. The suicide makes herself the judge in a matter not entrusted to her – God alone is the judge, it is his prerogative both to announce life and to pronounce death. 'There is no god besides me. I put to death and I bring to life ...' (Deuteronomy 32:39)".[19]

We see this self-centered thinking in the few suicide accounts recorded in the Bible:

Abimelech (Judges 9:50-54). Wanting

to be king, Abimelech hired assassins to murder his brothers and used military force against all who resisted him. At Shechem, he set fire to the city's tower and killed a thousand people who had sought shelter within its walls.

Employing a similar strategy at Thebez, Abimelech approached the tower to set it on fire. A woman dropped a millstone from the roof, cracking his skull. Seriously injured, Abimelech called to his armor-bearer to kill him. Apparently the shame of being killed by a woman motivated Abimelech to order his own death. "Hurriedly he called to his armor-bearer, 'Draw your sword and kill me, so that they can't say, 'A woman killed him.' So his servant ran him through, and he died" (Judges 9:54).

Samson (Judges 16). Mighty Samson died as a prisoner of the Philistines, the enemies of God's people. His capture provided an occasion for the Philistines to celebrate. Samson asked the Lord for strength to pull down the two central pillars of the temple, discrediting their deity and bringing death to thousands of Philistines. Samson died with them.

While Samson's death was self-inflicted, his death was not the primary purpose of his act. Ling notes, "the death of Samson was quite different ... Samson's death should therefore be seen, not as a suicide, but as an example of heroic self-sacrifice, exemplifying John 15:13, 'Greater love has no one than this, that he lay down his life for his friends.' Samson ended his days opposing the Philistine enemies of God. His intention was not to escape the difficulties of this life by suicide, but rather his death was a courageous giving of his life that others might live."[20]

In modern terms, Samson was the soldier who saves his friends by throwing himself upon a grenade. O'Mathúna concludes, "We can approve of those who sacrificially die for the good of others when no alternative exists. But we cannot approve of those who commit suicide for selfish reasons, or to escape pain or suffering, or because they see little hope in life. Admittedly this leaves some ambiguity, but this is where we must struggle with God's Word, the Holy Spirit's guidance, and the counsel of others as we seek to live and die in ways that glorify God (Romans 13:8; Philippians 1:20)."[21]

Saul (1 Samuel 31). King Saul, critically wounded in battle by Philistine archers to the extent that he could neither fight nor flee, made a request similar to that of Abimelech. He asked his armor-bearer to kill him. His armor-bearer wouldn't do it, however, and Saul fell on his own sword.

Saul feared the abuse of his enemies more than death itself (1 Samuel 31:4). Could God have delivered Saul from the Philistines as he later delivered Daniel's three friends from Nebuchadnezzar's blazing furnace? Shadrach, Meshach and Abednego had such trust in God that they saw both life and death as God's deliverance. They boldly said to the king, "If we are thrown into the blazing furnace, the God we serve is able to save us from it, and he will rescue us from your hand, O king. But even if he does not, we want you to know, O king, that we will not serve your gods or worship the image of gold you have set up" (Daniel 3:17-18).

Saul, however, was without faith, without hope, and without God. The official explanation of his death states, "Saul died because he was unfaithful to the Lord; he did not keep the word of the Lord and even consulted a medium for guidance, and did not inquire of the Lord. So the Lord put him to death and turned the kingdom over to David son of Jesse" (1 Chronicles 10:13-14).

Saul's armor-bearer (1 Samuel 31:5). Saul's armor-bearer refused to take his master's life, but he did not hesitate to take his own. "When the armor-bearer saw that Saul was dead, he too fell on his sword and died with him." Unlike Saul, the armor-bearer does not appear to have been wounded. He might have been able to flee. Or he might have gone down fighting. Or perhaps he could have survived being taken prisoner. Who can say for sure? But Saul's act both provided

an example and also gave permission to
the armor-bearer to handle his crisis in
the same way. That's why one suicide
is sometimes followed by a rash of
other suicides.

Ahithophel (2 Samuel 17). Ahithophel was
a trusted advisor to both King David and
Absalom, David's son. When Absalom
conspired against his father to make
himself king, Ahithophel joined the
younger man. However, when Absalom
rejected his counsel and David learned
of his betrayal, Ahithophel "put his
house in order and then hanged himself"
(2 Samuel 17:23). What Ahithophel did
calls attention to the orderliness of many
suicides. One woman cleaned her house,
placed her important papers on the
dining room table, wrote instructions to
her son, and posted a note on the garage
door saying where she could be found.
Then she called 9-1-1 and shot herself.

Zimri (1 Kings 16:9-19). Zimri became
king by murdering the man who trusted
him with half his chariots. Zimri had only

enjoyed royalty for seven days when the army learned how he had come to power. The soldiers in the camp immediately proclaimed their commander king and laid siege to the city where Zimri reigned. "When Zimri saw that the city was taken, he went into the citadel of the royal palace and set the palace on fire around him. So he died..." (1 Kings 16:18). Zimri was the Judas of the Old Testament. His name became synonymous with a servant who betrayed and murdered his master.

Judas (Matthew 27:3-5; see also Acts 1:18). Like Zimri, Judas betrayed his master, Jesus, to those who wanted to kill him. Judas was an apostle, hand-picked by Jesus to be with him throughout the course of his public ministry. He was trusted with the group's finances, but he was not a trustworthy man. John bluntly stated that "he was a thief; as keeper of the money bag, he used to help himself to what was put into it" (John 12:6). Scripture says that Judas betrayed Jesus for thirty pieces of silver (Matthew 26:14-16).

It is possible Judas did not think that

the chief priests would go so far as to put Jesus to death. Matthew recalls, "When Judas, who had betrayed him, saw that Jesus was condemned, he was seized with remorse and returned the thirty silver coins to the chief priests and the elders. 'I have sinned,' he said, 'for I have betrayed innocent blood'" (Matthew 27:3-4). When he understood the consequences of his actions, Judas felt badly. He felt *remorse*, but it was not the kind of sorrow that led him to *repentance*. Paul distinguishes godly sorrow from worldly sorrow. "Godly sorrow brings repentance that leads to salvation and leaves no regret, but worldly sorrow brings death" (2 Corinthians 7:10). Judas' sorrow did not lead him to seek forgiveness and reconciliation. Instead, "he went away and hanged himself" (Matthew 27:5). Acts 1:18 adds, "With the reward he got for his wickedness, Judas bought a field; there he fell headlong, his body burst open and all his intestines spilled out." Presumably, that occurred when his bloated body was found hanging and was cut down.

Men and Women Face the Same Issues Today

The issues that men and women faced then are the same issues men and women and teenagers face today. Broken relationships, betrayal, failure, guilt, shame, revenge, self-pity, pride, losses of various kinds and worldly sorrow still lead to death and suicide apart from the grace of God in Jesus Christ. "People today, struggling with suicide, still deal with the same issues: those of control and relationships. Real and perceived failures in these areas frequently bring someone to consider suicide, assisted suicide, or euthanasia."[22]

Suicidal friends lose hope and develop tunnel vision. They can see no other solution to their problem. But there is always another solution. Life does not need to end in tragic suicide. The Bible says, "No temptation has seized you except what is common to man. And God is faithful; he will not let you be tempted beyond what you can bear. But when you are tempted, he will also provide a way out so that you can stand up under it" (1 Corinthians 10:13).

The key idea here is that there is no problem that your friend faces that has not already been faced or is not being faced now by others. Your friend is not alone. We like to think that nobody has ever suffered like we have. "Is any suffering like my suffering?" (Lamentations 1:12). But that's not true. Have we suffered more than Job? More than the Apostle Paul? More than Jesus on the cross? The "way out" that God provides may not be easy, or what we want, but there is always an alternative to suicide.

Hebrews 11 speaks of men and women who faced unbelievable hardships and suffering, yet chose faith over death as the way out. That doesn't mean they never thought about dying or that death might be preferable to life. Some of them even prayed for God to take their lives from them.[23] These are the examples we should follow, not people like Saul, Ahithophel or Judas. "To depart this life by one's own choice is to reject the opportunity for loving and glorifying God in our bodies. We can do this through what we say and do, or through what others do for us. It can simply be our willingness to trust God and others in our final days. Rejecting suicide shows the willingness to accept God's sovereignty and grace and to depend on Him for direction. ... How we face death can be our final gift to those who survive us. This is how our lives and deaths can bring glory to God and take away the desire to hasten death."[24]

3

Help Your Suicidal Friend

If there are always solutions to life's issues that are preferable to suicide, what can you do to help your suicidal friend who is struggling to go on living? Because you are a caring person, "suicidal individuals will appear at your door whether or not you are prepared to deal with them."[25]

You Are Qualified to Help

You may not feel prepared, but you have what you need to help. Long before there were professional counselors, people in trouble relied upon family and friends to help them through difficult times. Writing to believers in Rome, the Apostle Paul said to the whole church (not just the church leaders[26]), "I myself am convinced, my brothers, that you yourselves are full of goodness, complete in knowledge and competent to instruct one another" (Romans 15:14). You possess three very important qualifications:

*You have the character to help others.
As a believer redeemed by Jesus Christ
and filled with his Spirit, you are "full of
goodness." You care about others and you
seek to do them good, not harm.*

*You have the knowledge to help others.
You may not know everything about the
problems your friend is confronting, or
be an expert on suicide, but you have
access to divine wisdom revealed in the
Scriptures. John Murray notes, "The
'knowledge' is the understanding of
the Christian faith..."[27] You are able to
discern what the revealed will of God
is and provide valuable guidance and
encouragement to your distressed friend.*

*You have the motivation to help others.
You are "competent to instruct one
another." The word translated "instruct" in
the NIV means to put or place into mind
and is elsewhere translated "admonish,"
"warn," or "counsel." It carries the idea
of lovingly confronting someone with
the purpose of bringing about desirable
change in his or her thinking and living.*

Your motivation for helping others is their welfare, not your own personal gain.

Warning Signs

With the right character, knowledge and motivation, you are able to actually help your suicidal friend. Three keys to preventing suicide are: Look, Listen, and Ask!

Look for signs of suicidal thinking! 70-75% of people who commit suicide tell someone about their plans. Warning signs may be both verbal and behavioral.

<u>Verbal signs include statements such as:</u>

"I wish I were dead."

"I feel like a big fat zero."

"I wish I had never been born."

"The world would be better off without me."

"I don't see any way to get out of this mess."

"Nobody cares if I live or die."

"I can't handle this."

"I can't live without _____."

"Life doesn't mean anything to me since..."

"You'll be sorry when I'm gone."

"Next time I'll take enough pills to do the job right."

<u>Some behavioral signs are:</u>

Dramatic mood swings

Loss of interest in normal activities; become quiet and withdrawn

Declining grades in school or productivity at work

Giving away possessions, pets

Fixation on death/suicide in writing or in pictures

Drug/alcohol abuse – drugs and/or alcohol are present in 56% of male and 68% of female completed suicides[28]

<u>Changes in personality</u>

Getting affairs in order (writing a will, paying off debt, unusual cleaning)

Evidence of planning, such as buying a weapon, rope, drugs or chemicals

While many people give clues that they are

suicidal, most observers do not recognize the signs until after the fact. That's when the pieces fall into place and the light goes on: "That's what he meant by that," and "That's why she gave away her kitten." Suicide-prevention educators should continue to teach the warning signs, but we cannot rely primarily on recognizing them in order to prevent suicides.

Listen to Your Friend

Listen to your suicidal friend! Be willing to talk about suicide plainly. Many suicidal people want to voice their thoughts, but their family and friends won't let them! You don't have to have all the answers; you just need to be willing to listen.

Take your friend seriously. Don't discount her concerns. Don't say, "It's not that bad..." To her it is! Don't tell her what to do, but show her biblically what God wants her to do. Help her to take every out-of-control thought and bring it into submission to Jesus Christ. "We demolish arguments and every pretension that sets itself up against the knowledge of God, and we take captive every thought to make it obedient to Christ" (2 Corinthians 10:5).

When in doubt, ask! If your friend's intentions

are not clear, ask him point blank: Are you thinking about suicide? It seems counter-intuitive, the opposite of what you think you should do, but asking will not push him to act. Talking about his thoughts and feelings may actually serve as a release-valve, thus buying more time.

Learn as much as you can about his suicide plan. A suicide threat assessment tool that I find helpful is easily remembered by the acronym SLAP DIRT[29]:

Specific plan – Has your friend thought about how, where and when he would commit suicide? A plan that is specific is much closer to being carried out than one that is only general: "I don't know how, but I'm gonna do it."

Lethality – How deadly is the plan? I'm not overly concerned about a plan to overdose on Vitamin C, but if someone says they're going to shoot themselves or jump from a freeway overpass, they have my full attention.

Availability (of means) – Does your friend have or can he easily get what he needs to carry out his plan?

Proximity (of help) – How close any help is can indicate determination. Fred moved in with his daughter and her family after his wife died. They were glad to have him there and

Fred did much of the gardening. One evening he said he was going for a walk. He actually went to a park in a neighboring city. In the gazebo in a remote part of the park, Fred put a handgun to his head and pulled the trigger. He went to an isolated place so that there would be no one nearby who could interrupt what he had decided to do.

If there has been a previous attempt(s), add **DIRT** to the mix:

Dangerousness – How dangerous were the previous attempts? Is there is a pattern of para- or pseudosuicidal attempts that were deliberately unsuccessful, and is your friend more determined now?

Impression – Whatever the actual danger might have been, what is your friend's impression of how dangerous her previous attempts were?

Rescue – How did your friend survive previous attempts? Did he use less than lethal means, or were there friends or other people who came to his rescue?

Timing – Some people attempt suicide expecting to be rescued. Linda rigged a vacuum cleaner hose from the tailpipe of her car in the garage into the passenger compartment, expecting her estranged husband to find her (and save her) when he came to pick up their children. She forgot he had a dentist appointment. As a result of that miscalculation, Linda died and almost killed her kids when carbon monoxide filled the house.

When depression is present, suicidal persons can send out conflicting signals. One of the most dangerous periods is on the way down, when they are unhappy with life and close to the bottom but still have enough energy to carry out a plan. At the bottom of the curve, life is flat and depressed persons have little energy to do anything. This is when they don't go to school or work, don't seem to get anything done, and spend a lot of time unable or unwilling to get out of bed or off the couch. When they start to come out of the depression that's the next most dangerous period because they are beginning to regain energy and can again carry out a plan. Often friends are misled into thinking that the suicidal person is getting better: "He seemed so much happier the last few days...." That apparent happiness may be because the person has a plan and now has the energy to carry it out.

Don't Try to Be a Hero

Suicide intervention is risky. It places you in harm's way, between a suicidal subject and the means of carrying out his plan. Your priority must always be your own personal safety first. Don't try to be a hero, and don't become a victim. Call for appropriate help from police, fire, or the local suicide crisis line.

I met Frank and Michelle on a domestic disturbance call. It was verbal only – no one was arrested. Officers separated the couple and I listened to both sides. They were arguing because Frank had come home drunk after he had promised that he would give up drinking. The situation settled down and we all returned to our other responsibilities. Later, I got a call at home on my cell phone. It was Michelle, who in panic told me that Frank had a knife to his throat and was threatening to kill himself! I asked her to put Frank on the line, and through tears he confessed that he was a rotten husband and a miserable human being who lied to his wife and failed to keep his promises. I asked Frank to get a notepad and pen so that he could write down some verses I would give him. Part of my reason for asking Frank to write things down was to get the knife out of his hand and de-escalate the threat. He set his knife on the kitchen counter and did as I asked. While he was getting a notepad, I alerted my wife to the situation and asked her to call police dispatch from our home phone. She stayed on the line with the dispatcher as I continued to talk to Frank. Officers staged outside Frank's apartment and prepared to enter on my word. By God's grace, that wasn't necessary. I was able to persuade Frank to leave his knife on the counter and go to the door to let the waiting officers in. Frank and Michelle went back to church together and received counseling from their pastor. Several years later, Michelle phoned to let me know they had moved to another state and were still doing well and walking with the Lord.

When intervening with a suicidal friend, there are some things to do and not to do.

SOME THINGS NOT TO DO:

Do not leave the person alone.

Do not overlook verbal and behavioral signs.

Do not sound shocked.

Do not interrupt while the person is still speaking – always be respectful and polite.

Do not make promises you can't keep; you will lose credibility and may never be able to help someone again.

Do not argue, and do not minimize what your friend says.

Do not debate morality – "Pointing out that suicide is sinful has limited value as a deterrent. However, as a way to explore the person's worldview, talking about suicide as sin is pure gold."[30]

Do not remain the only person helping – try to have someone else present.

Do not agree to keep this a secret – tell them that "confidentiality" means that they have confidence in you to do the right thing with the information they tell you.

Do pray without ceasing (1 Thessalonians 5:16-18).

Do remain calm – panic leads to mistakes.

Do be patient. Do not rush a suicidal person – slowing down her thoughts and behavior buys more time.

Do help to define the problem accurately.

Do rephrase thoughts for clarity and context.

Do focus on the central issue.

Do stay physically close to the person and secure the surroundings, limiting access to potential weapons.

Do emphasize the temporary nature of the problem – even if it's chronic or terminal, it's not eternal.

Do listen very carefully and respond appropriately.

If suicide is imminent or in progress, call 9-1-1 immediately!

Your friend came to you for help because she knows you're someone who cares. Don't let fear paralyze you. You might not feel qualified, but at that moment you're the best person for the job!

4

Hope for the Hopeless

While suicidal persons give many different reasons they may be considering ending their lives, the one common factor that all suicidal subjects display is the lack of hope. Therefore, the most effective way to remove suicide as a threat is to give hope to the hopeless.

What is hope? When we use the word "hope" in casual conversation, it often means little more than wishful thinking. "I didn't study, but I hope I get a good grade on the midterm!" "I hope that's not a police car behind me!" Such statements imply some degree of uncertainty about the future.

Hope is Rooted in Faith

When the Bible uses the word hope, however, it implies confidence about the future, not doubt. Jay Adams notes, "Hope in the Scriptures always is a confident expectation: the word hope never carries even the connotation of uncertainty that adheres to our English term (as when we say cautiously, 'I hope so')."[31] Faith and hope are related. "Now faith is being sure of what we hope for and certain of what we do not see. This is what the ancients were commended for" (Hebrews 11:1-2). The chapter goes on to describe the confident living of many different men and women who believed that the promises of God were true whether they saw them realized in their lifetime or not.

This is a very important observation for your suicidal friend. Where there is faith in God and his Word there is hope, and where there is hope, there is life. The writer continues, "All these people were still living by faith when they died. They did not receive the things promised; they only saw them and welcomed them from a distance" (Hebrews 11:13).

The opposite is also true: where there is no faith in God there is no hope, and where there is no hope, there is death. Perhaps the most haunting words in the Bible are Paul's description of people who are estranged from God. He says, "[R]emember that at that time you were separate from Christ, excluded from citizenship in Israel and foreigners to the covenants of the promise, without hope and without God in the world" (Ephesians 2:12).

Think about the spiritual and emotional

condition of those whom Paul describes. They are separate, excluded, strangers, without hope, and without God. This is the true condition of every one of us by nature.

False Hopes

Where can suicidal subjects find hope? Adams insists that suicidal persons "need hope. They are preeminently persons with no hope. Taking them seriously about their sin is absolutely essential. Hope comes when someone recognizes and acknowledges how hopeless the counselee is in his present situation. From agreeing that such a life is not worth continuing, the counselor can show the possibility of a new and different sort of life in Christ."[32]

If you are to help your suicidal friend you must know the answer to that question. Where can your friend find hope?

> *Not within himself.* Doug, a church youth group leader, tried to persuade Kevin not to commit suicide by telling him, "God sees you as lovable. He loves you with an everlasting love. He loves you no matter what you have done, no matter how

miserable your life is, no matter how big your problems are, no matter how many mistakes you have made or sins you have committed. God never stops loving you … and He never will."[33]

I don't ever want to minimize the greatness of God's love, but I think Doug's argument does exactly that. Doug wants Kevin to look deep within himself and see that there is something in him that deserves God's love. Doug shows that he doesn't fully understand the hopelessness and helplessness of Kevin's condition.

Kevin needs to look away from himself and focus on who God is. He needs to hope not in his own alleged self-worth or lovability, but in the truth that God loves sinners despite their sin! "But God demonstrates his own love for us in this: While we were still sinners, Christ died for us" (Romans 5:8).

Not in others. It should be evident that we are all sinners who fall short of the glory

God intends us to reflect as the bearers of his image.[34] It is not other people who give meaning to our lives and make life worth living: it is God who made us to glorify him and enjoy him forever.

Not in our circumstances. Sometimes we think, "Oh, if I only had such and such, then life would be worth living!" If we look to our circumstances to make life worthwhile, we will only be disappointed. Life is ever-changing. Friends come and go. Loved ones die. The "perfect job" turns out not to be perfect. We have injuries that do not heal and illnesses that cannot be cured. If we focus on circumstances, we will certainly find a multitude of reasons to be dissatisfied. But where there is faith in God and his Word there is hope, and where there is hope, there is life. Contentment is something that can be learned. Paul shared, "I have learned to be content whatever the circumstances. I know what it is to be in need, and I know what it is to have plenty. I have learned the secret of being content in any and every situation, whether well fed or hungry, whether living in plenty or in want. I can do everything through him who gives me strength" (Philippians 4:11-13).

Hope in Jesus Christ

Kevin needed to know that hope is knowing a person. Hope is knowing "Christ Jesus our hope" (1 Timothy 1:1). It is Jesus Christ, the eternal Son of God, who came into the world to save his people from their sin. It is the man Christ Jesus who perfectly kept the law on our behalf and so fulfilled all righteousness. It is Christ who offered himself as the propitiation or atoning sacrifice for our sins, thus fully satisfying divine justice and absorbing the wrath of God in his own body on the cross as our substitute. It is Christ who rose from the dead for our justification and sent his Holy Spirit into the world to give new life to spiritually dead sinners. It is Christ who is coming again for us at the end of the age in power and great glory and who promises to live with us forever. It is Christ who gives us hope and a future: "Now the dwelling of God is with men, and he will live with them. They will be his people, and God himself will be with them and be their God. He will wipe every

tear from their eyes. There will be no more death
or mourning or crying or pain, for the old order of
things has passed away" (Revelation 21:3-4).

How can suicidal persons find this hope? Paul
reminds us, "For everything that was written in
the past was written to teach us, so that through
endurance and the encouragement of the
Scriptures we might have hope" (Romans 15:4). The
word translated "encouragement" has the idea of
coming alongside to help. We cannot overestimate
the importance of the role of Scripture in helping
our suicidal friends to find a true and living hope.
It is not your love that will sustain them; it is
Christ's. It is not your power that will save them;
it is Christ's. It is not your wisdom that will change
their minds; it is Christ's. It is not your spirit that
will transform their lives; it is the Spirit of Christ.

Sometimes the officers I work with ask me how
I can continue to respond to such awful traumatic
events and how I can bear to share so much pain
and misery. I tell them it is only because I have
Christ-centered hope within me. The Apostle
Peter says, "But in your hearts set apart Christ as
Lord. Always be prepared to give an answer to
everyone who asks you to give the reason for the
hope that you have" (1 Peter 3:15).

That must be your answer, too. If you have a friend who is suicidal, your greatest privilege, and help to them, is to take them by the hand and introduce them to the One who alone is able to save completely all who come to him. Jesus said,

> "Come to me, all you who are weary and burdened, and I will give you rest. Take my yoke upon you and learn from me, for I am gentle and humble in heart, and you will find rest for your souls."
>
> (Matthew 11:28-29)

Conclusion

Your friend is suicidal. He is thinking about suicide and may even be threatening to take specific steps to end his life. Overwhelmed by the difficulties of life's circumstances, he has abandoned all hope. Tunnel vision has restricted the field of options and he can see only one way out. Death seems more appealing than life. You want to help but you're frozen in place, overwhelmed by the magnitude of his emotional distress.

Suicide is both delicate and dangerous. You're understandably afraid that if you make a wrong move or say the wrong words you could push your friend over the edge. In your mind, you could become responsible for his death. Suicide really is a matter of life and death. It's not something we are eager to confront.

Who will help your friend? You are no expert. My colleague in the church where we serve together spent many years physically building homes as well as spiritually building churches. He often says that the best tool is the closest tool that will do the job. You are there. The experts are not. You may need to call others to help, especially if suicide seems imminent. But while you're waiting for police, medics, or a counselor to arrive, you are the first responder.

This book has enabled you to see that you actually are able to help your friend and has given you some practical guidance in how to help. You bring a ministry of the loving presence of God, the encouragement of Scripture, and the promise of the Holy Spirit who is able to change lives to the most despairing hearts and into the darkest circumstances imaginable.

Christians are often hesitant to use our greatest resource, the Word of God. Paul Tripp explains, "In personal ministry, I want to bring more than a heart of compassion, a willingness to listen, and a commitment to help bear someone's burden. Though these are the sweet fruit of Christian love, I want to offer more. I want to bring the heart-changing truths of Scripture to people in the midst of their situations and relationships. Personal ministry is about people loving people, but in a way that includes bringing them God's Word."[35]

Don't use the Bible as just another self-help book. The gospel is a lifeline that God has thrown to save us by joining us to Jesus Christ by faith. He "is able to save completely those who come to God through him" (Hebrews 7:25). John Ling says it simply, "In the final analysis, the biblical direction for both the would-be suicide and the bereaved can be summed up in three words – go to God."[36]

Still scared? So am I! I have been responding to suicides for more than two decades and when I get into my car to respond to another call I still never know what I'm going to say when I get there. But I don't go by myself, and neither do you. Jesus encouraged his disciples, "Do not worry beforehand about what to say. Just say whatever is given you at the time, for it is not you speaking, but the Holy Spirit" (Mark 13:11). Christ has sent his Spirit into the world, and he helps us to help others. I may not know what to say, but I trust him to help me. You can trust him to help you, too.

Personal Application Projects

You picked up this booklet because you want to help people who are suicidal. Now you have finished reading it, but you are not done. You're just beginning...

» List the names of people you know who have committed or attempted suicide. Include family members, friends, coworkers, neighbors and acquaintances.

» How have the suicidal incidents above affected your life?

» What unbiblical thoughts and desires contributed to their decision to end their lives?

» What verbal and behavioral warning signs did you recognize?

» Your friend is also suicidal. What unbiblical thoughts and desires are influencing her?

» Depression can be a factor in suicidal thinking. Read Psalms 42 and 43. How does the psalmist combat depression? The writer seems to stand outside of himself and talk to his own soul. List the specific things he remembers and the directions that he gives to himself.

» Memorize Jeremiah 29:11-13.

» Discontentment is another significant factor in suicides. Memorize Philippians 4:11-13.

» Read Romans 8:18-39. How does a biblical understanding of God's sovereignty help suicidal people?

» Look up the hymn "God Moves in a Mysterious Way" by William Cowper in a hymnal or online. Now look up the story of how that hymn came to be written. Can reading and singing psalms, hymns and spiritual songs help suicidal subjects? See Ephesians 5:15-20.

» What do all suicidal people have in common? Memorize Romans 15:4 and 15:13.

» What can you do now to be more prepared to help your next friend who is suicidal?

Where Can I Get More Help?

BOOKS AND OTHER PUBLICATIONS

Adams, Jay E., *The Christian Counselor's Manual* (Nutley: Presbyterian and Reformed Publishing Company, 1973)

Black, Jeffrey S., *Suicide Understanding and Intervening* (Phillipsburg: P&R Publishing, 2003)

Bridges, Jerry, *Trusting God Even When Life Hurts* (Colorado Springs: NavPress, 1988)

Demy,Timothy J. & Stewart,Gary P., editors, *Suicide A Christian Response* (Grand Rapids: Kregel Publications, 1998)

Elliott, Harold, *Ripples of Suicide* (Waco: WRS Publishing, 1993)

Fitzpatrick, Elyse & Hendrickson, Laura, *Will Medicine Stop the Pain?* (Chicago: Moody Publishers, 2006)

Ling, John R., *The Edge of Life* (Epsom, UK: Day One Publications, 2002)

Lloyd-Jones, D. Martyn, *Spiritual Depression Its Causes and Cure* (Grand Rapids: Wm. B. Eerdmans Publishing Company, 1965)

Mack, Wayne, *Out of the Blues: Dealing with the Blues of Depression & Loneliness* (Bemidji: Focus Publishing, 2006)

QuickSeries (in collaboration with the International Critical Incident Stress Foundation), *Suicide Prevention* (Fort Lauderdale: QuickSeries Publishing, 2009)

Welch, Edward T., *Depression A Stubborn Darkness* (Greensboro: New Growth Press, 2004)

WEB AND OTHER RESOURCES

American Association of Suicidology, http://www. suicidology.org/home

Centers for Disease Control, http://www.cdc.gov/nchs/ fastats/suicide.htm

Crisis Hotlines – check online for local crisis hotlines and resources

The Institute for Biblical Counseling and Discipleship (IBCD), www.ibdc.org

The National Association of Nouthetic Counselors, www. nanc.org (for referral to biblical counselors in your area and other resources)

National Suicide Prevention Lifeline, 1-800-273-TALK (8255)

Many state and county Departments of Health (Medical Examiner or Coroner) publish annual reports online that provide helpful local information and statistics on suicide

Police and Fire Departments may have chaplains who are trained in crisis intervention and suicide. Check with your local department to see if they can help you with your suicidal friend or help provide training in your local church.

NOTES

1   The names and details of all incidents have been changed to protect the memories of those who died and to respect the privacy of those who lived.

2   Tomáš Masaryk, Modern Man and Religion (published posthumously in English, 1938).

3   David G. Myers, Psychology, 2nd Edition (New York: Worth Publishers, 1989), 456.

4   Centers for Disease Control, http://www.cdc.gov/nchs/fastats/suicide.htm, Accessed 04/06/2012

5   Community Health Improvement Partners, CHIP Report on Suicide in San Diego County, 1998-2007, vii.
    http://www.sdchip.org/media/53352/suicidedatareport_1998-2007.pdf, Accessed 04/06/2012.

6   Harold Elliott, Ripples of Suicide (Waco: WRS Publishing, 1993), title.

7   QuickSeries in collaboration with the International Critical Incident Stress Foundation, Suicide Prevention (Fort Lauderdale: QuickSeries Publishing, 2009), back cover.

8   Art Linkletter in Harold Elliott, Ripples of Suicide (Waco: WRS Publishing, 1993), foreword

9   Timothy J. Demy & Gary P. Stewart, editors, Suicide A Christian Response (Grand Rapids: Kregel Publications, 1998), 425

10 Gavin de Becker, The Gift of Fear (New York: Dell Publishing, 1997), 120

11 Some question whether Samson's death was a case of suicide or martyrdom

12 Nevada State Department of Health and Human Services, Nevada Suicide Prevention Plan 2007-2012, http://dhhs.nv.gov/Suicide/DOCS/2007-12NSPPOfficial.pdf, 24. Accessed 3/31/2012

13 Jeffrey S. Black, Suicide Understanding and Intervening (Phillipsburg: P&R Publishing, 2003), 8

14 Richard Bach, Illusions: The Adventures of a Reluctant Messiah, 1977

15 Linda Carroll, "Suicide risk spikes in week after cancer diagnosis, study finds", http://vitals.msnbc.msn.com/_news/2012/04/04/11022340-suicide-risk-spikes-in-week-after-cancer-diagnosis-study-finds?lite, Accessed 04/05/2012

16 http://apps.leg.wa.gov/rcw/default.aspx?cite=70.245, Accessed 04/05/2012

17 Dónal P. O'Mathúna in Demy & Stewart, Suicide A Christian Response, 349.

18 Thomas S. Szasz in The Antioch Review (1971), Cited in John R. Ling, The Edge of Life (Epsom, UK: Day One Publications, 2002), 118-119

19 John R. Ling, The Edge of Life, 112-113.

20 John R. Ling, The Edge of Life, 114.

21 Dónal P. O'Mathúna in Demy & Stewart, Suicide A Christian Response, 363.

22 Dónal P. O'Mathúna in Demy & Stewart, Suicide A Christian Response, 362.

23 See Rebekah (Genesis 27:46), Rachel (Genesis 30:1), Moses (Numbers 11:10-15), Elijah (1 Kings 19:4), Job (Job 6:8-13; 10; 13:14-15), Jonah (Jonah 4:3,8), and even Paul (2 Corinthians 1:8-10; Philippians 1:21-26).

24 Dónal P. O'Mathúna in Demy & Stewart, Suicide A Christian Response, 394-395

25 Timothy Tatum in Demy & Stewart, Suicide A Christian Response, 467.

26 Romans 1:7 "To all in Rome who are loved by God and called to be saints..."

27 John Murray, The Epistle to the Romans, Vol 2 (Grand Rapids: Wm. B. Eerdman's Publishing Company, 1965), 209.

28 CHIP Report on Suicide in San Diego County: 1998-2007, 10.

    http://www.sdchip.org/media/53352/suicidedatareport_1998-2007.pdf, Accessed 04/06/2012. While this report is specific to San Diego County, California, percentages reflect what is happening throughout the country

29 Chaplain Dan Nolta, Tacoma-Pierce County Chaplaincy. I received this tool in a suicide training conducted by Chaplain Nolta many years ago. Dan says he "stole" it from somebody else!

30 Jeffrey S. Black, Suicide Understanding and Intervening, 7.

31 Jay E. Adams, The Christian Counselor's Manual (Nutley: Presbyterian and Reformed Publishing Company, 1973), 39.

32 Jay E. Adams, The Christian Counselor's Manual, 45.

33 Josh McDowell and Ed Stewart, My Friend is Struggling with Thoughts of Suicide (Fearn,Tain, UK: Christian Focus Publications, 2008), 52

34 See, for example, Romans 1:18-32; Romans 3:9-20; Romans 3:23.

35 Paul David Tripp, Instruments in the Redeemer's Hands (Phillipsburg, NJ: P&R Publishing, 2002), 21

36 John Ling, The Edge of Life (Leominster, Day One, 2003), 122.

BOOKS IN THE HELP! SERIES INCLUDE...

(More titles in preparation)